LLAMAS

LIVING WILD

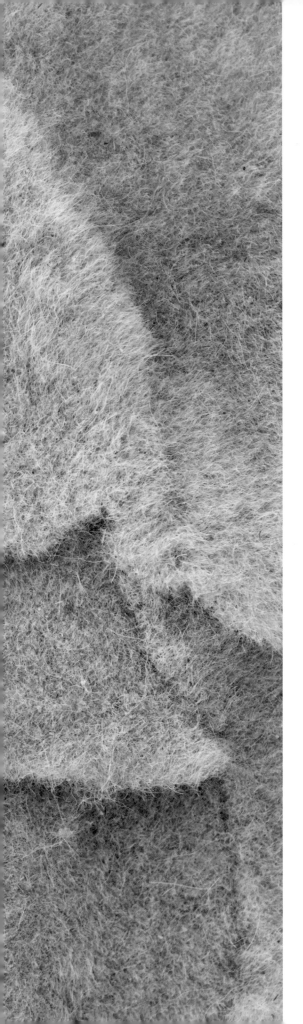

LIVING WILD

Published by Creative Education and Creative Paperbacks
P.O. Box 227, Mankato, Minnesota 56002
Creative Education and Creative Paperbacks are imprints of The Creative Company
www.thecreativecompany.us

Design and production by Mary Herrmann
Art direction by Rita Marshall
Printed in China

Photographs by Creative Commons Wikimedia (Plamen Agov, John Bourne 2009/ Walters Art Museum, Dr. John Finney/Brooklyn Museum, Liné1, Christophe Meneboeuf/pixinn.net), Dreamstime (Florian Blümm, Byvalet, Davthy, Peng Ge, Rob Hill, HOOKMEDIA Design, Ying Feng Johansson, Luckynick, Mirekdeml, Modfos, Hoang Bao Nguyen, Pixattitude, Patrick Poendl, Ginger Sanders, Nihar Shah, Evgeny Subbotsky, Toniflap, Martyn Unsworth, Kira Volkov, Gerald Voss, Weltreisendertj, Lucie Zrnova), iStockphoto (Generistock, GlobalP), National Geographic Creative (ERIKA SKOGG), Shutterstock (androver, Anastasiya Barbosova, belizar, Bildagentur Zoonar GmbH, Stefano Buttafoco, Edwin Butter, E.J. Johnson Photography, Helen Filatova, Diego Grandi, klublu, LFRabanedo, ostill, Larissa Pereira, Reel Hawks Studio, dubes sonego, Suzanne Tucker)

Library of Congress Cataloging-in-Publication Data
Names: Gish, Melissa, author.
Title: Llamas / Melissa Gish.
Series: Living wild.
Includes bibliographical references and index.
Summary: A look at llamas, including their habitats, physical characteristics such as their long necks, behaviors, relationships with humans, and their abundant domesticated population in the world today.
Identifiers: LCCN 2016036683 / ISBN 978-1-60818-831-4 (hardcover) / ISBN 978-1-62832-434-1 (pbk) / ISBN 978-1-56660-879-4 (eBook)
Subjects: LCSH: Llamas—Juvenile literature.
Classification: LCC QL737.U54 G573 2017 / DDC 636.2/966—dc23

CCSS: RI.5.1, 2, 3, 8; RST.6-8.1, 2, 5, 6, 8; RH.6-8.3, 4, 5, 6, 7, 8

First Edition HC 9 8 7 6 5 4 3 2 1
First Edition PBK 9 8 7 6 5 4 3 2 1

CREATIVE EDUCATION • CREATIVE PAPERBACKS

LLAMAS

Melissa Gish

In southern Peru's Moquegua region, a herd of llamas is grazing on the

Andean Plateau. The llamas' jaws move slowly, methodically chewing tender spring grasses.

In southern Peru's Moquegua region, a herd of llamas is grazing on the Andean Plateau. The llamas' jaws move slowly, methodically chewing tender spring grasses. The llamas gaze across the landscape, which seems to stretch endlessly toward the horizon. Far to the north stands the snow-capped peak of Mount Ubinas, a volcano towering 18,609 feet (5,672 m) tall. Young llamas prance around the herd, chasing each other playfully. Their mothers

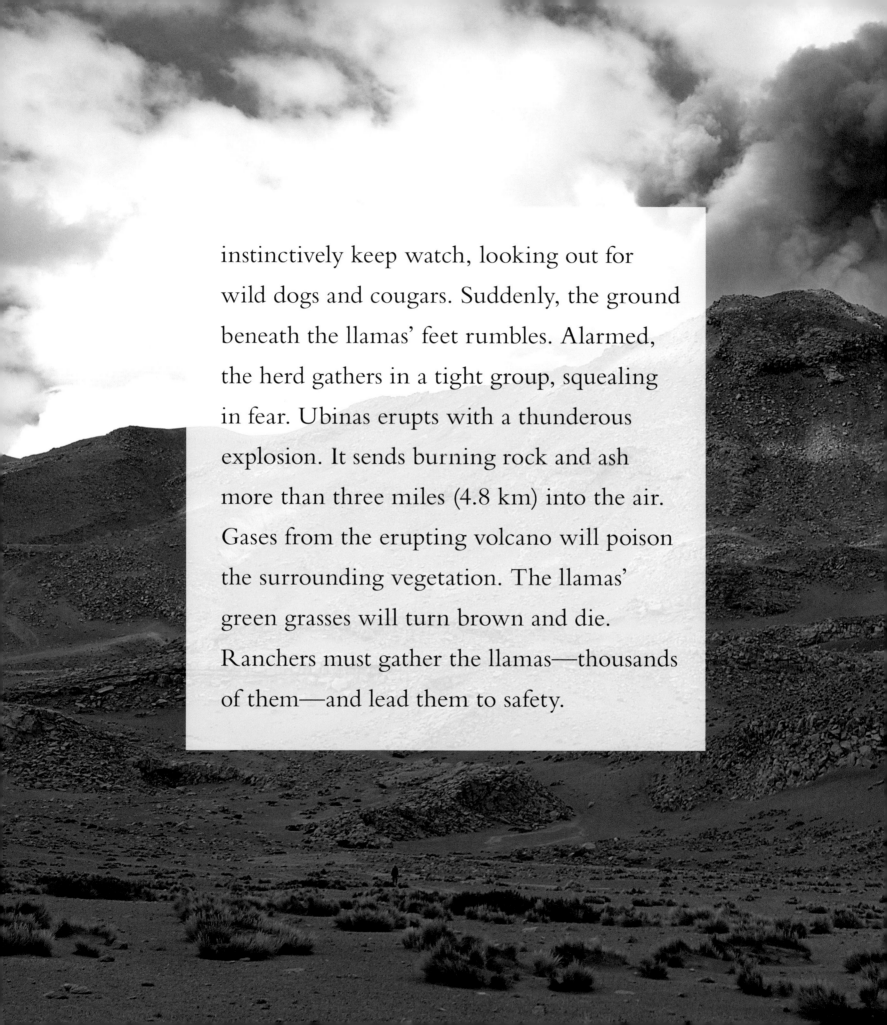

instinctively keep watch, looking out for wild dogs and cougars. Suddenly, the ground beneath the llamas' feet rumbles. Alarmed, the herd gathers in a tight group, squealing in fear. Ubinas erupts with a thunderous explosion. It sends burning rock and ash more than three miles (4.8 km) into the air. Gases from the erupting volcano will poison the surrounding vegetation. The llamas' green grasses will turn brown and die. Ranchers must gather the llamas—thousands of them—and lead them to safety.

WHERE IN THE WORLD THEY LIVE

■ **Llama**
domesticated herds in South America, ranches in North America

■ **Alpaca**
domesticated herds in southern Peru, northern Bolivia, Ecuador, northern Chile

■ **Guanaco**
mountain plains of Peru, Bolivia, Chile, Argentina

■ **Vicuña**
Peru, northwestern Argentina, Bolivia, northern Chile

Domesticated herds of llamas and alpacas are found by the thousands in South America, and some live on ranches and farms in North America as well. The wild lamoids, guanacos and vicuñas, are still native to South America, inhabiting mountain plains from Peru to Argentina. The colored squares represent general locations of each lamoid species today.

BUMP-FOOTED BEASTS

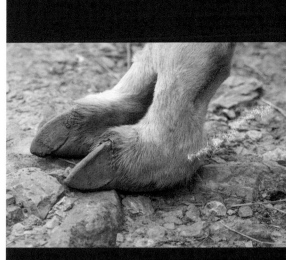

The skin between a llama's toes is loose, allowing the toes to spread apart, similar to the webbing on a duck's foot.

L lamas are members of the family Camelidae. The earliest camelids appeared in western North America about 40 million years ago. Most species were about the size of rabbits, and some stood on their hind legs to eat. About three million years ago, when some of these prehistoric animals were about the size of a goat, they moved south to escape one of Earth's ice ages. The camelids settled in the Andes Mountains in South America and became the group of animals called lamoids. This group includes the llama and guanaco in the genus *Lama* and the smaller alpaca and vicuña in the genus *Vicugna*. Larger prehistoric camelids traveled across the Bering **Land Bridge** to Asia, where they developed into the dromedary and Bactrian camels.

Lamoids and their Asian cousins make up the suborder Tylopoda, which means "bump-footed." These animals are characterized by thick, leathery pads on the bottom of their feet. The pads protect the feet from harsh terrain such as rock, hot sand, and ice. All bump-footed beasts have two toes. They look similar to the hooves of cows and pigs, but they are actually toenails that extend from

Alpacas have shorter ears and snouts than llamas, and they have thicker fleece on their foreheads.

About 28,000 llamas and alpacas were rescued from pastures around Peru's Ubinas volcano when it erupted in 2014.

the foot and curve downward. When llamas and their relatives walk over uneven terrain, their toes spread apart and their toenails dig into the ground for balance. Because footpads are more sensitive than hooves, llamas are more sure-footed than hoofed animals.

While the guanaco and vicuña have remained wild, around 3,000 years ago the Chavín people of what is now western Peru **domesticated** llamas and alpacas. The exact origin of the name "llama" (pronounced *YA-mah* by native speakers) is unknown, but 16th-century Spanish explorers adopted the name from the Quechua Indians of Peru.

Llamas and their relatives have long necks and small heads. People frequently mistake other lamoids for llamas because they look similar. Llamas and guanacos can grow up to four feet (1.2 m) tall at the shoulder. They may stand six feet (1.8 m) tall from head to toe. Alpacas and vicuñas are about 12 inches (30.5 cm) shorter. The llama can be distinguished from its lamoid relatives by its bulk. Llamas can weigh up to 450 pounds (204 kg)—nearly twice as heavy as guanacos and as much as four times the weight of alpacas and vicuñas.

Llamas vary in color, but all guanacos have light brown backs, white underparts, and gray faces with straight, slender ears.

A baby llama might not have the same coloration or pattern as its parents.

As mammals, llamas give birth to live offspring and produce milk to feed their young. Mammals are warm-blooded animals. This means that their bodies must work to maintain a constant healthy temperature that is usually above that of their surroundings. The llama's native habitat is the *Altiplano*, the grassy plateaus of the Andes Mountains at 10,000 feet (3,048 m) or more in elevation. The climate is cold, and the air has less oxygen than it does closer to sea level.

To withstand wind, snow, rain, and cold temperatures, a llama has two coats of fur. Close to the skin is a layer of thick, curly wool. On top of this undercoat are long, coarse guard hairs. These hairs trap warm air to **insulate** the llama's body core. The hair on the neck and body can grow up to eight inches (20.3 cm) long. Shorter hair covers the llama's head, underbelly, and legs to help keep it from getting too warm. Llamas vary in color from white, gray, and black, to brown, tan, and reddish. Some llamas are even spotted with a mix of colors.

Early llamas were prey for prehistoric predators, including the giant bear, scimitar cat, and dire wolf. As a result, llamas developed keen hearing with their long,

Llamas have substances in their blood that help them live at high altitudes where there is less oxygen.

A llama can swivel its ears and lay them back to detect sounds from nearly all directions without moving its head.

banana-shaped ears. A llama's large eyes are set far apart, so it can see almost all the way around itself. The eyes are shielded by a double row of thick eyelashes that not only protect the llama's eyeballs from rain, snow, and dust, but also provide shade from the sun. Like a cat's whiskers, the llama's eyelashes are sensitive to touch. They can detect objects close to the eye, which is useful when llamas are browsing for food among trees and bushes. A nictitating (*NIK-tih-tayt-ing*) membrane (a see-through inner eyelid) closes over the llama's eyes for added protection.

Llamas are herbivores, which means that they eat only plants, leaves, grasses, seeds, and fruits. The llama has a **prehensile** upper lip. Split down the center, the lip has two halves that are able to move independently, and, like gripping fingers, are useful for grabbing vegetation and pushing it into the mouth. Llamas normally have 30 or 32 teeth, but they have no front teeth in their upper jaw. They rip plants using the sharp front teeth in their lower jaw and the hard gums of their upper jaw. Then llamas grind the food using their back teeth, called molars.

When male llamas are about two years old and females are about four years old, they develop fighting teeth. These

The llama's tongue and two upper lips function together to work grassy food into its mouth.

If a llama's teeth grow unevenly, its keeper might trim its front teeth straight to make sure it can eat properly.

are similar to the canine teeth in dogs and cats, except llamas have two pairs on the top and one pair on the bottom. In females, these teeth are short, but in males, they can be more than one inch (2.5 cm) long. The fighting teeth are curved and very sharp. Male llamas will use the teeth to fight each other, sometimes causing serious injury. Therefore, llama keepers routinely have the fighting teeth cut down to stubs, which does not hurt the llamas and prevents them from hurting each other.

A special stomach with three chambers allows llamas to eat grasses and twigs that many other animals cannot digest. Food passes through the first chamber, called the rumen, where bacteria and acids soften it. Then the food is regurgitated, or brought back up to the llama's mouth. This food mass, called a cud, is chewed again. When it is swallowed, the cud passes through all three stomach chambers to be fully digested. Llamas share this trait of cud chewing, or ruminating, with animals such as giraffes, sheep, and cows. These other animals, which have four stomach chambers, are called ruminants. Llamas and their relatives are known as modified ruminants because they have only three stomach chambers.

Ruminants, such as sheep, as well as modified ruminants (such as llamas and camels) chew cud for about eight hours per day.

Although fully domesticated today, llamas have kept their wild defensive instinct to watch for predators.

HAPPY HERDS

L lamas have not lived in the wild for thousands of years. Long ago, humans found that llamas, being calm and curious, are easy to train. Roughly seven million llamas and alpacas are found in domesticated herds in South America, and more than 200,000 llamas live on ranches and farms throughout North America. Llamas have become known around the world for their meat, wool, and ability to carry up to 25 percent of their body weight. On farms and ranches around the world, male llamas are kept as guard animals to lead and protect smaller livestock from coyotes, foxes, and other predators. When a llama detects a predator, its posture stiffens, alerting others in the herd. Then it emits a special alarm cry. The instinct to protect its herd—despite the species in the herd—drives a guard llama to run toward the predator, kicking out and placing itself between the intruder and the livestock. Llamas are capable of killing dangerous dogs and coyotes.

Llamas are highly social and intelligent animals that thrive in herds. With individual personalities, some llamas are very calm, while others are nervous.

Because llamas can't support weight directly on their spines, they must carry loads in special packs over their rib cages.

Like dogs and horses, llamas have individual temperaments and personalities that their keepers easily recognize.

Llamas typically drop their dung in community heaps— researchers think this is perhaps done to mark the herd's boundaries.

Personalities are developed partly by **genetics** and partly by the llama's environment and treatment by human handlers. Occasionally, domesticated llamas are abandoned by their owners. Without the company of humans or other animals, these llamas may become **feral**. Organizations such as Wild Earth Llama Rescue in Taos, New Mexico, seek out feral llamas, which are often frightened and in poor health. Many organizations work to find the llamas new homes; some take the animals in themselves. Feral llamas can be re-socialized with domestic llamas, but they are typically distrustful of people for the rest of their lives.

Long ago, wild llamas had to compete for sparse food resources high in the cold Andes Mountains. The instinct to protect food and water remains in llamas today. In a llama herd, male llamas are instinctively driven to establish and maintain a territory large enough to provide adequate grazing for the herd. A dominant male marks his territorial boundary with piles of **dung**. He will battle other males by kicking and biting. The best way to keep male llamas safe from each other is to surgically alter some of them so they cannot breed. Llamas that have had

this surgery are called geldings. A dominant, breeding male is known as a stud or sire.

A dominant male llama must control the size and makeup of his herd. If he feels that there is not enough food to go around, he will kick out some of the members. Dams, or females that have had at least one offspring, are often preserved in the herd. Baby llamas are called crias (*KREE-uhz*). When crias become old enough to breed, the dominant male will chase them away. Eventually they form their own herds. This also helps prevent inbreeding and overpopulation. Llama ranchers typically break up their herds into smaller groups that establish separate

The Ecuadorean town of Saquisilí hosts one of that country's largest outdoor markets, with everything from food and crafts to llamas.

Adorning llamas with colorful decorative items is part of a centuries-old Peruvian tradition.

territories, or they trade llamas with other ranchers to safeguard their herds' bloodlines.

Even the calmest llama is always on alert. Llama behavior can switch in an instant from relaxed to tense or even hostile. They do not like to touch each other, particularly on the face or head. Bumping, kicking, biting, and spitting are all acts of aggression. Llamas do not like to be touched by people, either. Though they are generally calm around humans, llamas tend to turn away or move out of reach when handled. Despite this instinct to avoid touch, llamas can tolerate human contact with training as they build a relationship and come to trust their keepers. Although llamas learn to respect their keepers, they do not exhibit affection like dogs and cats do.

Llamas are quiet most of the time, but they do have a variety of vocalizations. Most commonly, llamas hum to themselves and to others. Dams and crias hum to each other to bond. The tone of humming may change depending on a llama's mood. A soft hum, combined with forward-leaning ears, indicates contentment or curiosity. A louder hum combined with ears pulled back signals irritation. Along with a clicking tongue or snort,

On frosty mornings high on the plateau, llamas must step through the ice on shallow streams to drink the water.

Llamas usually drink about two to three gallons (7.6–11.4 l) of water per day but may drink less if their food is moist.

Llama mothers remain watchful of their offspring, caring for them and protecting them, for their first year of life.

this hum may say to another llama, "Don't get too close to me." When upset or fighting with each other, llamas scream and squeal loudly. The llama's alarm call sounds like a deep, rasping laugh. This warns others in the herd to be alert and ready to respond to a threat. While breeding, males make a gurgling sound called orgling.

Llamas have no specific mating season. In cold climates, ranchers usually prefer to breed llamas in the spring so crias can grow up in the warmth of summer. Llamas are capable of breeding at six to nine months of age. However, responsible keepers typically allow llamas to reach full maturity before allowing them to breed. For females this is about two years old, and for males, about three years old. After a **gestation** of 11.5 months, a single cria is born. Twins are rare, and often one or both crias do not survive. A newborn typically weighs 25 to 30 pounds (11.3–13.6 kg). It can walk within an hour of being born and begins feeding on its mother's milk within two or three hours. The cria will stay close to its mother for five or six months, until it no longer requires her milk.

Llamas prefer to graze naturally in green pastures. In colder climates, however, ranchers must provide additional

grass or alfalfa hay. A llama eats about 2 percent of its body weight in dry plant matter each day. A 400-pound (181 kg) llama could eat up to 8 pounds (3.6 kg) of food every day. Many keepers also feed their llamas specially formulated llama pellets. These pellets look like dry dog food and are typically made of corn, wheat, and alfalfa as well as various vitamins and minerals. Pellets are high in **nutrients**, so llamas need to eat only one to two cups (0.2–0.5 l) of pellets per day. With good care, including **vaccinations** and treatment for **parasites**, llamas can live up to 30 years.

The backward position of a mother's ears communicates that others should keep their distance.

The rocks depicting llamas on the walls at the Incan site of Choquequirao were set in place more than 500 years ago.

MYSTERY AND MAGIC

Sculptures such as this (created 800 years ago) show the importance of llamas to the Andean peoples.

Llamas are one of the most important animals in the **cultural** history of many **indigenous** peoples of the Andes Mountain region. Similar to the relationship that North American Plains Indians had with bison, the ancient Andean civilizations relied on llamas for their livelihoods. The Moche civilization arose about 2,000 years ago in northern Peru. In the dry valleys between the Andes and the Pacific Ocean, the Moche used llama dung to fertilize their crops. Llamas had been domesticated for a thousand years and served the Moche as pack animals. Their hides provided warm clothing and blankets, and their meat fed the people.

The Moche were expert craftsmen. Their gold jewelry, woven rugs, and pottery often depicted birds and animals—including llamas. In 1987, Peruvian **archaeologist** Walter Alva discovered the tomb of a Moche king dating to the second century A.D. Many artifacts were found there, as were the skeletons of a dog and two llamas. According to folklore, the dog would have guided the king to the afterlife, and the llamas' meat would have fed him on his journey.

Incan conopas *are only about 3 inches (7.6 cm) long; this was carved more than 500 years ago.*

Llamas spit at each other to show dominance or chase intruders away from food, but they rarely spit at people.

When the Moche civilization faded away in about A.D. 800, it was replaced by the Muchik people. In 2010, American **anthropologist** Haagen Klaus led a team of researchers to an archaeological site known as Cerro Cerrillos, or Mount Cerrillos, in southern Peru. There, Klaus studied the remains of more than 80 children who had been killed as blood sacrifices. Ritual killings such as these were common among the ancient peoples of the Andes. Llamas played a significant role in the ceremonies. Some rituals were held to form political alliances, and some served to please the gods. At Cerro Cerrillos, llama meat was set aside as gifts to the sacrificed children. The belief was that the children would eat the meat in the afterlife. The remaining llama meat was served as the main course at great feasts that celebrated the sacrifices. Pure white llamas were selected for these rituals.

By the time the Inca Empire emerged in the 13th century, llamas and alpacas were considered sacred animals. The killing of these animals outside of planned rituals was punishable by death. The Inca people continued depicting llamas in pottery, jewelry, and fiber art. Small stone figurines, called *conopas*, were shaped like

llamas and alpacas, and little openings in their backs were stuffed with offerings to the god Urcuchillay. He was depicted as a colorful llama who watched over animals. Filled with materials believed to be magical, such as animal fat, seashells, corn, and the leaves of cocoa plants, the conopas were buried in pastures inhabited by llamas and alpacas. Urcuchillay would then protect the herd and encourage the animals to breed. Large, healthy herds equaled great wealth for llama and alpaca herders.

In 1992, American **archaeozoologist** Dr. Jane Wheeler discovered 26 perfectly preserved 1,000-year-old alpaca and llama bodies. They were found among

The Inca believed that white llamas, called paq'os, *talked to holy men and gave prophecies of the future.*

CHOQUEQUIRAO

The Inca royal estate and ceremonial complex, Choquequirao is perched majestically at 9,800 feet of elevation on the cloud-forested ridge of a glaciated 17,700-foot peak....

It is a truly "lost city," abandoned sometime around 1572 when the holdout last Inca ruler, Tupac Amaru, was captured in the distant jungles, dragged back to Cusco, and executed by Spanish colonial authorities. The ancient houses, temples, canals, and walls were soon reclaimed by the silent, green, primeval forest, only to be rediscovered and revealed in recent times. Located on the far, unpopulated and geographically hostile side of the immense Apurimac Canyon, the region remained disconnected from the farms, villages, and roads of developing Peru....

During the height of the Inca empire, 1450–1526, both Choquequirao and Machu Picchu would likely have served as a provincial administrative center.

There is reasonable evidence that Machu Picchu and Choquequirao may have also provided a seasonal pilgrimage destination for regional state-sponsored ceremonial events.

Evidence that coca was widely grown, coca store houses, llama pens, and a unique llama train mural, support Choquequirao as an important coca growing and distribution center. Intensive cultivation, ongoing construction, and maintenance would have required a large resident population. Remains of a large settlement of simple, round, wood dwellings contained by low stone walls is situated over an area of several square miles, above an outlying temple water shrine, Pinchaunuyoc. These would have housed the needed workers well away from privileged resident Inca administrators, attendants, and main group temples.

From a 2015 article by Gary Ziegler for the Andean Air Mail & Peruvian Times

the ruins of an ancient village in Peru called El Yaral. Mummified by the region's dry climate, the animals were in such good condition that even their eyelashes remained. Wheeler found that the alpaca's wool was much softer than modern alpaca wool. The Inca people were master weavers, and alpaca and llama fabrics were used as currency among tribes.

People of the Inca Empire built stone walls and structures in and around their cities and **shrines**. The ruins of Choquequirao, a late 15th-century holy place, still stand in southern Peru. Although the site had been explored many times from the 18th to the 20th century, it wasn't studied until American archaeologist Gary Ziegler led a team there in 1992. Ziegler believes this was a sacred place where high priests and other leaders gathered to perform rituals. A major feature of the site is the *quilcapirca*, which means "rock art on wall." Walls arranged like enormous steps and decorated with images of llamas were built on the mountainside. Twenty-four llamas and one human are depicted on the stone walls. Varying in height from about four to six feet (1.2–1.8 m), the llama herd appears to be guided by the human figure.

The best-quality wool comes from the back, upper sides, and rump, called the blanket area, of a llama or alpaca.

The llama's soft undercoat is used for handicrafts and clothing, while long, coarse guard hair is used to weave rugs and ropes.

An alpaca's fleece weighs an average of three to four pounds (1.4–1.8 kg), while a llama's can weigh nearly twice as much.

Llamas can catch parasites from deer, including brain worms, which grow in the animal's brain and spine and cause death.

Today, llamas are still used as pack animals in Peru, Bolivia, and neighboring countries. Tourists visit ancient sites such as Choquequirao and Machu Picchu accompanied by llamas that carry their water and gear. In North America, llamas are not only raised as guard and pack animals, they are also used for pure enjoyment. Rowanwood Farm in Sandy Hook, Connecticut, is a licensed llama hiking company. Hikers can lead llamas on a two-mile (3.2 km) trek through Paugussett State Forest—simply for the fun of it. Owner A. J. Collier says, "Just walking your own llama is magical."

With small heads and long legs and necks, llamas are comical looking animals. They lend themselves well to stories and animation. Llama Llama is a beloved character created for young children by author and illustrator Anna Dewdney. Her book *Llama Llama Red Pajama* (2005) launched a collection of books featuring llama characters. In the 2000 Walt Disney movie *The Emperor's New Groove*, spoiled teenager Emperor Kuzco is magically turned into a llama. The experience helps him see the world in a new way and become a much nicer person when he regains his human form. The Nickelodeon

Movies production *Jimmy Neutron: Boy Genius* (2001) features Jimmy's best friend, Carl Wheezer, as a card-carrying member of the Llama Love Society. He even rides a pet llama.

Swan Mountain Llama Trekking, in northwest Montana, is the oldest llama hiking organization in the United States.

Caminandes (which means "path") is a series of short, animated films created in 2013 by three friends. They used free software and shared the videos online, alongside tutorials that show viewers how to make their own movies. The first episode, *Caminandes: Llama Drama*, features a hapless llama trying to cross a busy highway. In the second episode, *Caminandes: Gran Dillama*, the llama discovers a delectable berry bush but finds an electric fence stands in his path. Both films are on YouTube as well as Caminandes.com, where fans can learn more about the movies and their makers.

Ropes made of camelid hair are lighter and stronger than other fiber ropes, and they repel moisture.

LEARNING FROM LLAMAS

Spanish explorers first set foot in Inca territory in 1526. By 1572, Spain had conquered the Inca Empire, stealing its wealth and destroying its culture. Thousands of llamas were killed and replaced with sheep, horses, and donkeys. Many Inca people were enslaved, but some fled to the high mountains, where they carried on the tradition of llama herding. The Spanish also began hunting the llama's cousins, the guanaco and vicuña, for their fine wool. Over the next 400 years, these animals, once numbering in the millions, were hunted nearly to **extinction**. Conservation efforts began in the 1970s, when only a few thousand guanacos and vicuñas remained. Today, the llama's cousins are still struggling, mainly because of illegal hunting.

Llama populations, however, have remained strong over the centuries, thanks to breeders in Ecuador, Peru, Bolivia, Chile, and Argentina. Until the late 20th century, llamas were considered exotic animals and kept in zoos in North America. In 1972, Richard and Kay Patterson purchased llamas to breed at Walnut Valley Farms in Ohio. Within 4 years, they had more than 500 llamas. The Pattersons

The traditional relationship between llamas and people remains strong among the people of the Andes.

Dams produce only about two ounces (59.1 ml) of milk at a time, so crias must feed frequently to get enough nutrients.

Llamas will refuse to carry loads that are too heavy for them by lying down or even kicking their keeper.

marketed llamas as domestic livestock and assisted in the forming of the Llama Association of North America (LANA) and the International Llama Association (ILA).

Since llamas are not native to North America, they are not as easy to raise as sheep or cattle. By the mid-1980s, though, farmers and ranchers were breeding and raising llamas by the thousands as working animals and for their wool. The American Llama Show Association (later renamed to the Alpaca and Llama Show Association) was formed in 1986 to put together competitions where llamas and alpacas are exhibited, and breeders are awarded prizes. Today, llamas typically sell for anywhere from $2,000 to $10,000 depending on quality. Because of their luxurious wool, alpacas can sell for as much as $50,000. Many youth groups such as 4-H, FFA, and Boy and Girl Scouts have llama programs, and llamas are routinely included in county and state fair livestock shows.

Research on llama breeding and care continues today. Some research involves the creation of hybrids, or mixed-breed animals. Since llamas, alpacas, and camels all share genetic properties, they can interbreed. The offspring of a llama and an alpaca is called a *huarizo*. The idea is to get the

Peruvian traditions of decorating llamas and alpacas have been adopted in U.S. parades and festivals, too.

Llamas roam freely at historic sites such as Machu Picchu, where tourists can delight in watching their natural behavior.

soft wool of the alpaca on a larger animal. The offspring of a llama and a camel is called a cama. Camas are meant to increase the llama's size, since dromedary camels can be up to six times as big as llamas. The results of interbreeding have been mixed. Huarizos typically turn out fine, but camas are often stubborn and difficult to train.

Medical research involving llamas is also widespread. Dr. Laura McCoy of the Scripps Research Institute in California is studying the antibodies of llamas as tools to combat human disease. Antibodies are substances in the blood that fight infection and disease caused by bacteria and viruses. Some diseases are too powerful for the body to eliminate. Llamas have special antibodies that naturally work against HIV. Researchers are trying to find a way to use these antibodies in humans. Because llamas are very different from humans, their antibodies must be modified to work in human bodies. But if they are successful, the researchers will be able to help people fight HIV.

Dr. Alejandro Balazs of the Ragon Institute is also studying llamas. The Ragon Institute is a research facility in Massachusetts dedicated to finding vaccines for diseases of the immune system, particularly HIV and **AIDS**. Vaccines help antibodies work better. Balazs studies how llama antibodies mutate, or change, in response to exposure to HIV. With each exposure, the antibodies get stronger and work better. Balazs wants to develop a vaccine from llama antibodies. He believes it will one day be possible to give people a series of vaccinations—each one making the person's antibodies stronger than before—until they become immune to HIV.

Scientists at the Texas Biomedical Research Institute in San Antonio have discovered that llama antibodies are also useful in fighting botulism. Botulism bacteria can grow in improperly preserved or spoiled food. When a person eats the infected food, the bacteria attack the

Peruvians traditionally label their llamas and alpacas with ear tassels to mark the animal's gender, owner, and village.

Ranchers and llama keepers must make sure that the hay they feed llamas is dry, as fungus growing on moist hay can be deadly.

nervous system, often causing death. Governments around the world worry that botulism could be used as a biological weapon, so the search for treatments is important. Llamas could hold the key, as their antibodies are immune to seven different kinds of botulism bacteria.

In another healthcare arena, llamas are being used to simply make people feel better. Researchers have long known that therapy animals can improve the well-being of children, the elderly, the mentally challenged, and the sick and injured. Therapy llamas are popular all across North America. In Vancouver, Washington, Mtn Peaks Therapy Llamas and Alpacas provides the gentle, woolly beasts for visits to senior communities, hospitals, rehabilitation facilities, and schools. Since 2007, operators Shannon Hendrickson and Lori Gregory have made hundreds of visits throughout British Columbia, Washington, and Oregon. The star of the show, a brown llama named Rojo, even has his own Facebook page.

Animal husbandry is the science of breeding animals to pass along the best qualities of both parents to their offspring. Llama husbandry may be geared toward creating intelligent guard animals. Studies have shown

that when a few llamas are mixed in with a herd of sheep, attacks by coyotes and wild dogs are rare. Other llamas are bred to have the best wool. Llama wool is sheared every two years. It's like getting a very close haircut and does not hurt the animal. The weight of a llama's woolly coat, called fleece, is about 6.6 pounds (3 kg). The wool is made into yarn, which can sell for more than $100 per pound! Llamas have served humans for thousands of years. They have long been an important part of rural Andean life and are now valued for their many uses. Llamas' unique personalities and behaviors continue to fascinate and entertain people around the world.

A skilled shearer can shear a llama in about 15 minutes, leaving an inch (2.5 cm) of wool on the llama's blanket.

ANIMAL TALE: HOW THE LLAMA CAME TO BE

About half of Peru's current population is descended from the Inca people. Bits and pieces of Inca culture and traditions still survive today, including this folk tale that explains how the llama came to be and why it serves humans.

Long ago, during the time of Inca, there lived a king with many beautiful daughters. The king's daughters spun and wove goat hair to make cloth and rugs. This skill was greatly admired, and the king's daughters took pride in their work. But the youngest and most beautiful of the daughters grew weary of spinning and weaving. She longed for adventure.

One night, the princess climbed over the city wall and sneaked into the forest. It seemed magical: frogs singing, night birds calling, and insects buzzing. Entranced by the wonder of the forest, the princess did not see the panther ready to pounce. Suddenly, a figure came crashing through the trees and chased the deadly cat away. The princess was terrified, but then she realized that a man had saved her.

She thanked him, and as the two walked back to the city, they talked and laughed, enjoying the beautiful twilight together. They promised to meet again, and they did—every night for many weeks. Soon they decided to marry. The princess introduced the man to the king, hoping to gain his approval for the marriage.

But the king was furious. He felt betrayed by his daughter. As punishment for their disobedience and secrecy, the king ordered the two lovers killed. The princess's mother was horrified. She begged her husband for mercy. The king, recalling the foolishness of his own youth and the joys of young love, took pity and spared the young lovers. Instead of death, he banished them to the highest mountain farthest from their home.

After a time, the king's wife could stand it no longer. She sent a magic bird to check on her daughter. The bird reported that the lovers were living in misery. The rocky earth tore their feet, they suffered cold wind, and they found little to eat. Saddened, the king's wife called upon Viracocha, the loving creator god, and asked him for help.

Viracocha had a difficult decision. He understood the foolish choices of the young lovers, but he also understood the king's decision. Viracocha could not erase the punishment, but he could change it. He turned the lovers into a pair of tall, sturdy creatures with feet that could walk easily over the rocky earth, thick wool that kept them warm against the wind, and an appetite for the dry grass that covered the mountainside.

When the king learned of the strange new creatures living in the faraway mountains, he demanded to see them. They were brought to the city, and the king immediately recognized his daughter's soft, brown eyes. Angry with his wife for going to Viracocha, but also very glad to be reunited with his daughter, the king made a compromise. He decreed that the two creatures be put to work carrying heavy loads. Their wool would also be sheared and given to his other daughters in place of goat hair. They would spin and weave the finest garments for the king. To this day, the descendants of the Inca still use llamas in these ways.

GLOSSARY

AIDS – a disease that causes the failure of many body systems and weakens the body's ability to fight off illness

anthropologist – a scientist who studies the history of humankind

archaeologist – a person who studies human history by examining ancient peoples and their artifacts

archaeozoologist – a person who studies the bones, shells, hair, and other items an animal leaves behind when it dies

cultural – of or relating to particular groups in a society that share behaviors and characteristics that are accepted as normal by that group

domesticated – tamed to be kept as a pet or used as a work animal

dung – waste matter eliminated from the body of an animal

extinction – the act or process of becoming extinct; coming to an end or dying out

feral – in a wild state after having been domesticated

genetics – relating to genes, the basic physical units of heredity

gestation – the period of time it takes a baby to develop inside its mother's womb

indigenous – originating in a particular region or country

insulate – to protect from the loss of heat

land bridge – a piece of land connecting two landmasses that allowed people and animals to pass from one place to another

nutrients – substances that give an animal energy and help it grow

parasites – animals or plants that live on or inside another living thing (called a host) while giving nothing back to the host; some parasites cause disease or even death

prehensile - capable of grasping

shrines – places associated with a holy person or thing

vaccinations – substances given to provide protection from diseases

SELECTED BIBLIOGRAPHY

Bonavia, Duccio. *The South American Camelids*. Translated by Javier Flores Espinoza. Los Angeles: University of California, 2008.

Cebra, Christopher, David E. Anderson, Ahmed Tibary, Robert J. Van Saun, and LaRue W. Johnson. *Llama and Alpaca Care: Medicine, Surgery, Reproduction, Nutrition, and Herd Health*. St. Louis: Elsevier, 2014.

Encyclopedia of Life. "*Lama glama*: Llama." http://eol.org/pages/309018/details.

Greater Appalachian Llama and Alpaca Association. "Learn About Llamas and Alpacas." http://www.galaonline.org/learn.html.

National Geographic. "Llama: *Lama glama*." http://animals.nationalgeographic.com/animals/mammals/llama.

Portman, Charles. University of Michigan Museum of Zoology. "*Lama glama*: Llama." Animal Diversity Web. http://animaldiversity.org/accounts/Lama_glama/.

Note: Every effort has been made to ensure that any websites listed above were active at the time of publication. However, because of the nature of the Internet, it is impossible to guarantee that these sites will remain active indefinitely or that their contents will not be altered.

Llamas normally avoid face touching, but sometimes they are overcome by curiosity and must investigate each other closely.

INDEX